Fact Finders®

→HOW LONG DO STARS LAST?

BY EMILY HUDD

CONTENT CONSULTANT
Edward Churchwell, Professor
Emeritus, Department of Astronomy,
University of Wisconsin–Madison

CAPSTONE PRESS
a capstone imprint

Fact Finders Books are published by Capstone Press,
1710 Roe Crest Drive, North Mankato, Minnesota 56003
www.mycapstone.com

Library of Congress Cataloging-in-Publication Data
Names: Hudd, Emily, author.
Title: How long do stars last? / by Emily Hudd.
Description: North Mankato, Minnesota : Capstone Press, 2020 | Series: How
    long does it take? | Audience: Grade 4 to 6. | Includes bibliographical
    references and index.
Identifiers: LCCN 2019000186 (print) | LCCN 2019002139 (ebook) | ISBN
    9781543573022 (ebook) | ISBN 9781543572964 (hardcover) | ISBN
    9781543575415 (pbk.)
Subjects: LCSH: Stars--Evolution--Juvenile literature.
Classification: LCC QB806 (ebook) | LCC QB806 .H83 2020 (print) | DDC
    523.8--dc23
LC record available at https://lccn.loc.gov/2019000186

All internet sites appearing in back matter were available and accurate when this book was sent to press.

Editorial Credits
Editor: Marie Pearson
Designer and production specialist: Dan Peluso

Photo Credits
iStockphoto: Pitris, cover (sun); NASA: ESA, 18, ESA/GSFC, 27, 29 (supernova), ESA/Hubble/GSFC, cover (stars),
Goddard/SDO, 14, 29 (main sequence), Hubble Heritage Team/GSFC, 24, 29 (planetary nebula), JPL-Caltech,
23, 29 (white dwarf), 29 (neutron star), 29 (black hole), JPL-Caltech/ESA, the Hubble Heritage Team STScI/
AURA and IPHAS, 8, 29 (protostar), JPL-Caltech/STScI, 7, 29 (nebula); Science Source: Davide De Martin, 17,
29 (red giant), John Chumack, 20, Mark Garlick, 10–11, Mark Garlick, 29 (black dwarf); Shutterstock Images:
Pozdeyev Vitaly, 13, Yuriy Kulik, 5

Design Elements: Red Line Editorial

TABLE OF
CONTENTS

STARGAZING

It is winter. A girl and her family are bundled up. They are looking at constellations. A constellation is a group of stars that ancient observers thought looked like animals, people, and other things. These people named the shapes. The girl's dad points out Orion. Orion is a hunter in Greek legends. He is a strong warrior holding a sword. In the Orion constellation, three stars in the middle make Orion's belt. The star on Orion's leg is the seventh-brightest star in the sky.

The girl notices some stars are red. Others are blue or white. Stars with different colors are different temperatures. Stars have life cycles that can last for billions of years!

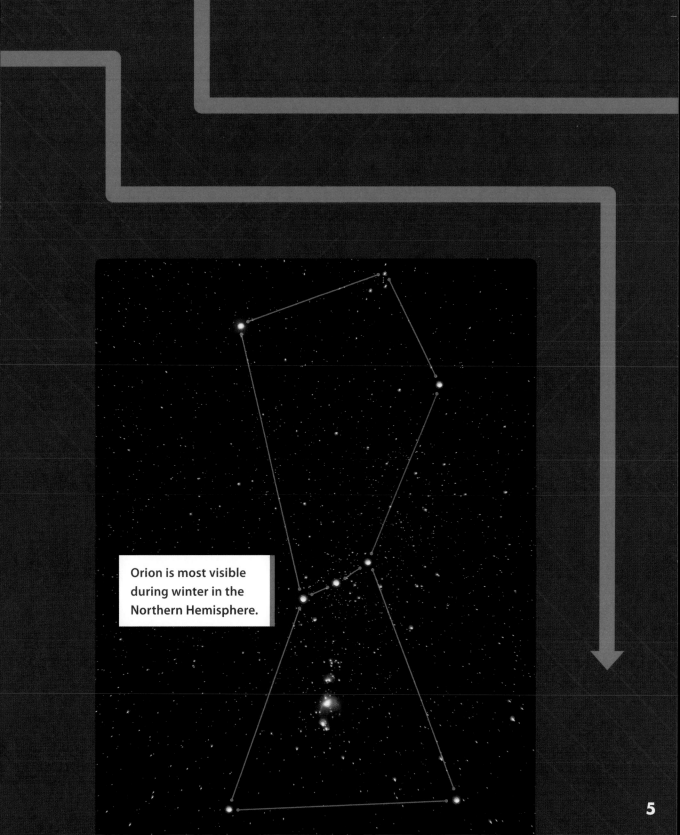

Orion is most visible during winter in the Northern Hemisphere.

CHAPTER ONE

HEATING UP

People can see some large objects like stars and planets from Earth. What they don't see is what lies between the objects. Outer space is not empty. Dust and gas float through space. Nebulas are clouds of gas and dust. Stars are born in nebulas. **Gravity** pulls gases and dust together. This forms a clump of **dense** gas called a protostar. Protostars are not yet stars. This is the first stage of the star life cycle. The clump grows, and pressure on the clump's center increases. This pressure makes the center very hot. This center is called the core.

gravity—a force that pulls objects with mass together; gravity pulls objects down toward the center of Earth

dense—when the matter that makes up an object is packed tightly together

Nebulas come in many colors and patterns.

A protostar grows in a cluster of gas and dust called the Tadpole.

Gravity continues to pull dust and gas, including **hydrogen**, into a ring around the protostar. As gas falls onto the protostar, the protostar spins. The core gets hotter. The star begins to glow. It spins faster as it gathers **matter**.

Big protostars grow faster than small stars. They spin quickly and pull in lots of gas and dust at faster speeds. Big protostars can form in 1 million years. Smaller ones take longer to form. They spin and grow slower. It can take them more than 100 million years to form.

FACT

Astronomy is the field of science that studies stars and outer space.

hydrogen—a natural gas that is found on Earth in the air

matter—any substances that make up objects or living things in the world and outer space

The ring of dust and gas around a protostar forms outer layers around the core. The layers are joined to the core by gravity. Gravity pulls gas into the core.

FACT
The sun is slightly larger than the average star. It formed in about 50 million years.

A protostar pulls in gas from the nebula around it.

The layers put more pressure on the core. The core gets even hotter.

Growing is an important part of a star's life cycle. A star's **mass** determines how long it will live and how it will die.

mass—the amount of matter in something

BRIGHT STAR

When a protostar's core reaches 15 million degrees Fahrenheit (8 million degrees Celsius), it becomes a star. In this second stage of life, the star is called a main sequence star. It shines brightly because of the core's high temperature and **density**. Hydrogen fuels the core. There is more hydrogen in the universe than any other energy source. Gravity and heat cause hydrogen to **fuse**. This turns hydrogen into the gas helium. The process produces lots of light.

FACT

The process of hydrogen turning into helium in a star's core is called nuclear fusion.

People can see some stars from Earth. But there are many more stars that are too far away to be seen with the naked eye.

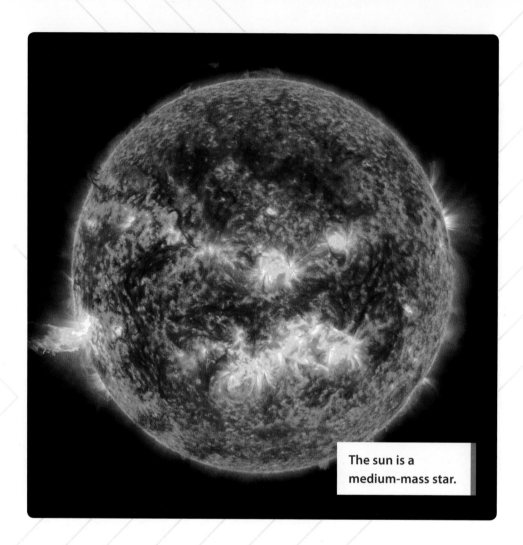

The sun is a medium-mass star.

The light shines brightly. People can see some stars from Earth.

Stars spend 90 percent of their lives as main sequence stars. This stage is the longest in the star's life cycle. It can last for millions or billions of years.

Stars with a large mass live shorter lives than lower mass stars. They use up their hydrogen quickly. Small stars live longer because they use energy slower. They can live for billions of years.

BRIGHTEST STAR IN THE SKY

Sirius, or the dog star, is the brightest star in the night sky. It is part of the Canis Major constellation, which is shaped like a dog. Sirius is a main sequence star. It shines a blue-white color. It is the brightest star people can see in the night sky because it is very close to Earth. It is 8.6 **light years** away.

light year—the distance light travels in one year; it is equal to 5.9 trillion miles (9.5 trillion kilometers)

CHAPTER THREE

RED GIANT

Eventually, all the hydrogen in the star's core gets used up. It has been turned into helium. The core shrinks, but the outer layers expand. The lower layers are so hot that they push the outer layers away. The star grows wider.

This is the third stage of the star. It is a red giant. It is named for how it looks. It is larger than before. It glows red. This is because the temperature in the outer layers is lower than that in the core. The outer layers form a bright shell of gas around the central star.

FACT
Stars expand to more than 400 times their original size as red giants.

Betelgeuse is a red giant star. It is in the constellation Orion.

The star cools. It is a red giant. It can swallow matter or planets nearby as it swells.

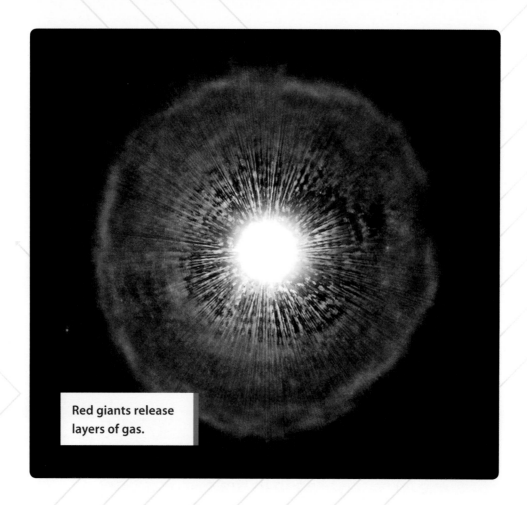

Red giants release layers of gas.

The sun will engulf Mercury and Venus as a red giant. It may even reach as far as Earth. But this will not happen soon. The sun will not become a red giant for another 5 billion years.

STAR RANKINGS

Stars are classified by mass and temperature. There are seven different groups. Each group is represented by a letter. Group M includes the coolest stars. Then, groups K, G, F, A, and B get hotter. Group O contains the largest and hottest stars. Additionally, stars in each group can be ranked zero to nine for finer temperature divisions. Zero is the hottest temperature. The sun's classification is G2.

During the red giant stage, the star continues to give off energy. There is no more hydrogen in its core. It uses hydrogen from its outer layers instead. All the hydrogen in the layers turns into helium.

Once all the hydrogen in the core is changed to helium, the star needs a new energy source. The star's core gets hotter. It becomes hot enough to burn helium as fuel. It starts with the helium in the core. The helium turns to **carbon**.

carbon—a natural substance that is found on Earth in rocks and all living things

A star's temperature determines its color. A star changes colors throughout its life. Usually it starts as yellow and white. Most main sequence stars range from red for the lowest mass stars to yellow to white to blue for the most massive. When stars cool, they turn to orange or red.

Arcturus is a red giant in the constellation Boötes.

The surface temperature of blue stars is more than 54,000 degrees Fahrenheit (30,000°C). White and yellow stars range from 18,000 to 11,000 degrees Fahrenheit (10,000 to 6,000°C). Red stars are less than 5,000 degrees Fahrenheit (3,000°C).

The red giant stage happens at the end of the star's life. Most stars spend the last 10 percent of their lives as red giants. The red giant stage is shorter than the main sequence stage because helium burns faster than hydrogen. The star can use up all the helium in a few thousand years. As the helium runs out, the outer layers shrink. All stars evolve in the same way during the red giant stage. What happens next depends on the star's mass.

CHAPTER FOUR

DWARF OR
SUPERNOVA

A star's life comes to an end after the red giant phase. It has burned all of its fuel. A star's mass determines how it will die. A star with medium or low mass becomes a white **dwarf star**. This includes stars that are the size of the sun. In the first step, the outer layers of the star become planetary nebulas. They form at the end of the red giant phase. When the red giant shrinks, it casts off its outer layers into space. These are planetary nebulas.

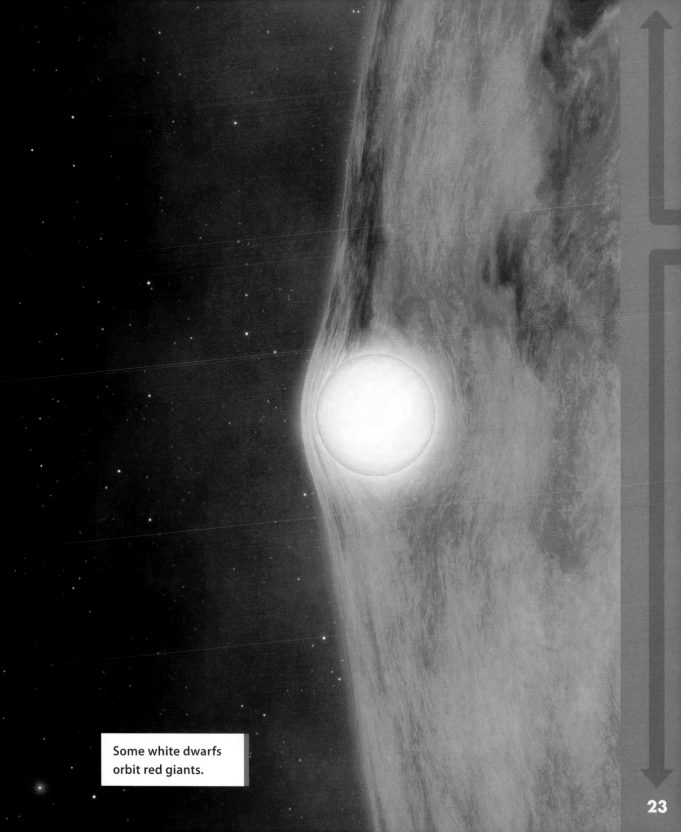

Some white dwarfs
orbit red giants.

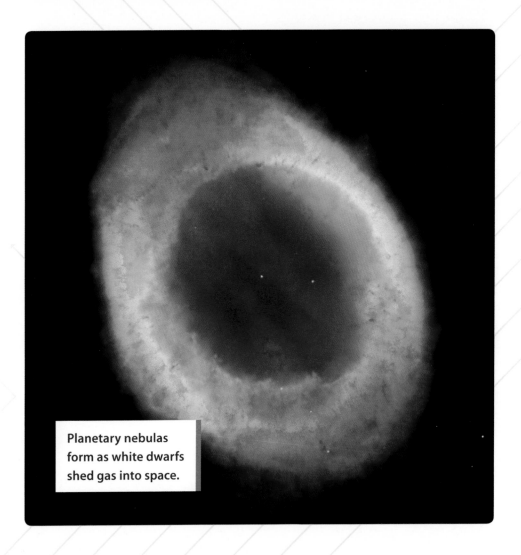

Planetary nebulas form as white dwarfs shed gas into space.

Planetary nebulas live short lives compared to stars. For tens of thousands of years, they are scattered in space.

Sometimes they glow because they are absorbing energy from the star they were part of. Planetary nebulas continue the star life cycle.

Eventually, all the star's layers drift into space. Only the core is left. It is very hot and shines brightly. The core is now a white dwarf star. White dwarfs are made of carbon and **oxygen**. They are a similar size to Earth, but very dense. A spoonful of this matter would have about the same mass as Mount Everest. This is the last stage for low-mass stars that scientists have seen.

FACT

The surface of white dwarfs can be more than 180,000 degrees Fahrenheit (100,000°C). They are some of the hottest stars in space.

oxygen—a gas that is used for many things on Earth, including breathing and breaking things down

However, scientists think there is another stage after white dwarfs. A white dwarf slowly cools and dims. All its energy goes away. It stops shining and turns dark. It is a black dwarf. Scientists think it could take trillions of years for a white dwarf to cool and become a black dwarf. The universe is only 13.8 billion years old. So none have formed yet.

Massive stars take a different path after the red giant stage. They may become **supernovas**. Supernovas are explosions. An explosion happens when a red giant star runs out of fuel.

At the end of the red giant's life, there is no more energy to support the star.

FACT
The core temperature of a star right before a supernova is more than 100 billion degrees Fahrenheit (555 million°C).

supernova—a stage in the star life cycle where a star explodes at the end of its life

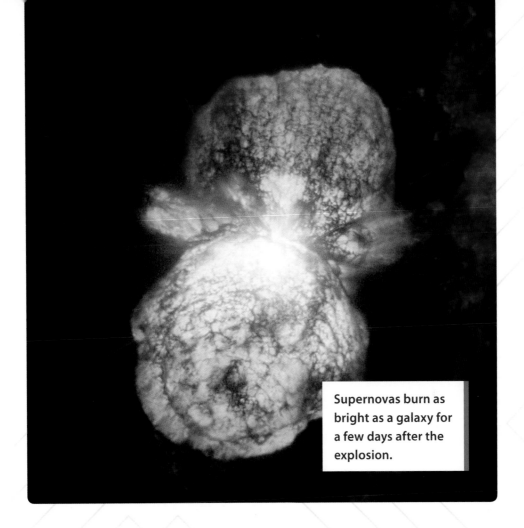

Supernovas burn as bright as a galaxy for a few days after the explosion.

In less than a second, gravity causes the outer layers to cave in. This causes a powerful supernova explosion. Dust and elements are blasted far into space.

The dense core of the supernova is left after the explosion. It will become a **neutron star** if its mass is less than two to three times that of the sun. This is the last stage for massive stars. The explosion causes the neutron star to spin quickly. It can spin several hundred times per second.

If the star is more than two to three times as massive as the sun, it becomes a black hole. Black holes are the rarest end for stars. After the explosion, the black hole has strong gravity. The gravity pulls everything toward the black hole. Scientists can't see what is in black holes. Even light is sucked in.

FACT

Neutron stars are more dense than white dwarfs. A neutron star that is only 12 miles (20 km) across could weigh as much as two suns.

neutron star—a very dense star that is the result of the collapse of a much larger star

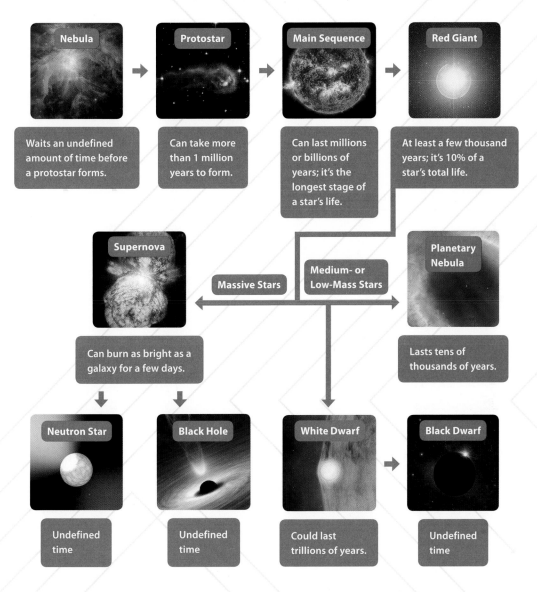

Stars have an amazing life cycle. They can last millions or billions of years.

GLOSSARY

carbon (KAHR-buhn)—a natural substance that is found on Earth in rocks and all living things

dense (DENS)—when the matter that makes up an object is packed tightly together

density (DENS-i-tee)—the measure of the weight of an object compared to its size

dwarf star (DWORF STAHR)—a star with smaller than usual size and mass

fuse (FYOOZ)—to combine multiple things together

gravity (GRAV-i-tee)—a force that pulls objects with mass together; gravity pulls objects down toward the center of Earth

hydrogen (HYE-druh-juhn)—a natural gas that is found on Earth in the air

light year (LITE YEER)—the distance light travels in one year; it is equal to 5.9 trillion miles (9.5 trillion kilometers)

mass (MAS)—the amount of matter in something

matter (MAT-ur)—any substances that make up objects or living things in the world and outer space

neutron star (NOO-trahn STAHR)—a very dense star that is the result of the collapse of a much larger star

oxygen (AHK-si-juhn)—a gas that is used for many things on Earth, including breathing and breaking things down

supernova (SOO-pur-noh-vuh)—a stage in the star life cycle where a star explodes at the end of its life

ADDITIONAL RESOURCES

FURTHER READING

Carlson Berne, Emma. *Totally Wacky Facts About Planets and Stars*. Mind Benders. North Mankato, Minn.: Capstone Press, 2016.

Drimmer, Stephanie Warren. *Night Sky*. National Geographic Readers. Washington, D.C.: National Geographic, 2017.

Rhatigan, Joe. *Space: Planets, Moons, Stars, and More!* Step into Reading. New York: Random House, 2016.

Spilsbury, Richard. *Space*. Adventures in STEAM. North Mankato, Minn.: Capstone Press, 2019.

CRITICAL THINKING QUESTIONS

1. What is the difference between protostars and main sequence stars? Use evidence from the text to support your answer.

2. After the red giant stage, a star can die in different ways. In your own words, describe the path a star can take when it dies.

3. The star life cycle can last millions or billions of years. Would you want to live as long as a star? Why?

INTERNET SITES

DK Find Out! What Is a Star?
https://www.dkfindout.com/us/space/stars-and-galaxies/what-is-star/

NASA Space Place: What Is a Supernova?
https://spaceplace.nasa.gov/supernova/en/

National Geographic Kids: Star Parties
https://kids.nationalgeographic.com/explore/space/star-parties/#starry-night.jpg

INDEX

ABOUT THE AUTHOR

Emily Hudd is a full-time children's author who loves writing nonfiction on a variety of topics. She lives in Minnesota with her husband.